DAVID POLAK

Fortify Your Mind

How To Conquer Temptation and Defeatism In a World of Weakness and Excess

This book was professionally typeset on Reedsy.
Find out more at reedsy.com

Contents

Preface

The 21st century man and his reason to continue his purpose, has fallen to a state never seen in all of human history. His drive for purpose and meaning has been torn down ever so slowly but also so sharply that he has resorted to self-hatred and societal despondency. Men whose fathers help build castles and empires now fail to build the mental foundations necessary to achieve them. I believe we are born conquerors of our own dreams and ambitions but we've been raised like we were the ones conquered and we are therefore weakened physically, mentally, and spiritually for it.

Why in this age of technological advancement has this happened to countless young men like me, to find themselves caught in the swamp of nihilism and its inevitable ideology of suicidal thinking? Why is it so easy nowadays to drown yourself in social media distractions, instead of searching for our own life's purpose and meaning?

Why is lust and perversion much more present and accepted around young men?

But most importantly, why must you **Fortify Your Mind**?

1

What to Expect From This Book

The main goal of this book is to lay out the foundations and basics of self-improvement to men that have fallen to addiction, nihilism, loneliness, or worsening mental health. I aim to help you rebuild your mental strength and reason for better living in a fast and easy way that could be done immediately after setting the book down. Most of the information in this book is my knowledge and opinions with actual facts and statistics mixed in here and there. I intend to give everyone a clear understanding of what exactly my interpretation of 'fortifying' your mind is and why it is necessary to achieve it.

What I mean when I say to 'fortify' your mind, I'm not saying to block people out or to contain your feelings, I mean it as an analogy to help you resist negative or tempting feelings that may be present in your day to day life.

I'll also be going over the ways men try to escape from reality with video games or waste their time to cope with their struggles and lack of purpose. Lastly, this book is mainly for men that have to practice self-improvement entirely alone with minimal or support from friends and family, since many of us suffer in silence and don't have the opportunity to get external support.

2

Mindfulness and Contentment In The Present Moment

"Man is affected not by events but by the view he takes of them" – *Epictetus*

Men that have their thoughts control what they think will have those same thoughts control how they act; becoming slaves in their own mental kingdom. They don't understand how mere **sensations** are corrupting their minds because they do not understand that they **are** just mere **sensations**. Men of the 21st century either overthink or do not think enough because they do not have good mental health and their routines reflect it and further reinforce it everyday. Men nowadays find it remarkably easy to seek pleasure, addiction, and attention on social media which just eats away slowly at their minds causing them to be emotional and have child-like interests that only succeed at holding them back from their true potential.They misunderstand or just ignore the highly beneficial and somewhat rare opportunity of feeling perfectly content in the present moment; to be alone but not lonely, and relaxation without screen time distractions.

"You have power over your mind - not outside events. Realize this, and you

will find strength." – Marcus Aurelius

Take a second to close your eyes and visualize your brain as your own personalized kingdom complete with walls that protect you from temptation, a treasury that represents your animal brain (subconscious), and trade routes that process information that you consume through your eyes and ears everyday. Understand that the information that you **consume** daily shapes **what** you think and **how** you think of yourself. Now, look back at what you've recently been seeing and hearing throughout your life for the past week or month and self reflect on one significant bad habit that you would like to change overall. Identify the causes and begin to write down a small simple goal that you think would best assist you in achieving that goal. Stay consistent by incorporating it into your daily routine by marking it down in your journal everyday. Lastly, list all the things that you are grateful for and celebrate the small positives that happen to you on a daily or weekly basis. Yes, something as small as smiling to a stranger is a positive that should be celebrated. Once you get the ball rolling, you'll feel as if you are leveling up in a game because your mind isn't actively working against you anymore with dangerous mental health problems at the front gates. Don't let the mind's ills hold you back.

The Importance Of Meditation

Meditation is one of the most **important** yet seemingly underrated practices in modern life. The simple act of just sitting down in a comfortable position without your phone or music playing, and just closing your eyes for 5-10 minutes a day is the secret of why so many people that do it can focus and be productive without their minds distracting them with negative thoughts.Meditation does not even have to be for 5-10 minutes, it can be for 1-2 minutes, or even 30 seconds, as long as you do it everyday it is a **victory**.

While you meditate, be **content** with how you feel in the **present moment** whether your thoughts are raging or calm, just focus on the breath and **visualize** your thoughts being washed away with water. The art of letting your mind wander and regaining the focus of your breath already starts to rebuild the broken foundation of the castle wall you have broken down in your subconscious. This is the first step to put you back in charge of your newfound mental kingdom.

Meditation can also help deal the finishing blow on addiction. Addiction itself (with substance abuse/pornography/or a habit that is difficult to stop) is just a pychological sensation that drives you to physically act on it to temporarily sedate the craving while "rewarding" you with a unnatural sense of pleasure and euphoria to keep you as its slave. Simply focus on the craving, and wash it out of your thoughts by concentrating on the rhythm of the breath. I recommend doing this multiple times in every meditation session.

"Sensations may drive how you feel and what you do, but you still hold the steering wheel." – Author

"Your life is what your thoughts make it." – Confucius

3

Break Beyond The Shackles of Stress Life

I believe that the 21st century is the most mentally challenging century that mankind has ever had to face without a doubt. Average stress levels in this modern age eclipses all any other time in human history, with more and more men and women joining the workforce, stressful jobs with long hours, and higher inflation every year makes people very worried about how they are going to put food on the table, or how they are going to get out of their painful 9-5 job. Men's mental health has fallen to such a low point, many of them actually came to believe that their gender isn't needed or even wanted anymore in the current society. Which results in suicide.

According to the American Foundation for Suicide Prevention,

- The suicide rate is highest in middle-aged men
- Firearms are the most common method of suicide deaths in 2020
- Men died by suicide 3.88x more than women in 2020
- On average, there are about 130 suicides per day
- Currently, suicide is the 12th leading cause of death in the US

I cannot tell how **unequivocally vital** it is for men today more than ever to fortify their minds in all given respects, because most of the time, if your mind is overly stressed every single day, it will lead to path of suicide. You can't always control the circumstances that make you stressed, but you **can** and **must** control how you **respond** to them.

Prioritize your mental health above all else

For short term stress relief I recommend:

- Get in touch with creativity
- Long walks or jogs
- Reading a book
- Family vacation
- Working out

For long term stress relief I recommend:

- Meditation
- Goal setting
- Balanced diet
- Gratitude journaling
- Get a hobby

Struggling to keep a 9-5 type job for a family of 3 forever isn't your mission in life. It exists so you can rise above it.

Even when a king is seriously stressed out, he has ways to deal with it so that he doesn't put his people in more danger than they already are. The

21st century man **Copes** with his stress by turning to unhealthy habits that only help to **forget** his current pain after work everyday. He starts smoking, drinking too much, goes to parties, escapes to video games, and eats junk food etc. If the king thought like a slave, based his actions like a slave, and deals with stress like a slave, he would then become a slave.The king understands that he alone has the sole **responsibility** to protect his kingdom from outside enemies, he knows that if his thoughts aren't working **for** him, then it's working **against** him, which is what the enemy wants. It is the same literally and figuratively, **weak minds don't create strong kingdoms.**

People may say, "but we're not kings leading an entire kingdom of people that's constantly being tested by outside forces." Well in the literal sense yes, but I obviously never meant it to be that way. You're all kings. In your mind, you must be the one that turns an everyday bad situation (9-5 grueling work day) that you can't escape from, into a life of self- discovery of your own **purpose**, with the little free time that you possibly have. A king must sacrifice his comfort today for a more prosperous tomorrow. Thats what makes kingdoms grow and expand. It's the **difference** between the **king** and the **slave.**

"Happy is the man who has broken the chains which hurt the mind and has given up worrying once and for all." – Ovid

"The secret of happiness, you see, is not found in seeking more, but in developing the capacity to enjoy less" - Socrates

4

Your Body Needs to Rest

According to the Sleep Foundation,

- "35.2% of all adults in the US. Report sleeping on average for less than seven hours per night."
- "Around 75% of adults with depression suffer from insomnia."
-
- "Adults between 18 and 64 **need seven to nine hours of sleep** per night."

If you're not getting **7-8 hours of sleep per night**, you are not giving your mind and body the time to properly **recover** from the day's events. "Resting" means that you are sleeping, not watching shows on TV or playing video games until 1:00 in the morning. If you don't get enough sleep for reasons like that, then you're making your life way harder than it ever had it be. Everyone's muscles would forever be weak if they didn't take their sleep seriously. One of the most important aspects of **decision making**, **muscle recovery**, and **increased concentration** throughout the day starts with **good nightly rest**. At the start of everyday, it is you who lifts yourself out of bed to show your new found appreciation for life and its gifts that it has created, so make the most out of it.

If you're having trouble sleeping, I recommend:

- Make your bedroom as dark as possible (Shut off all light)
- Wear a sleep mask
- Sleep medication that works (For insomnia or sickness)
- Make your bedroom cool but not cold for easier sleep
- Sleep on your side (more comfortable)
- Meditate before sleep (to clear persistent thoughts)

5

Mental Fortitude and Dopamine Detox

A spire to be like Mt.Fuji, with such a broad and solid foundation that the strongest earthquake cannot move you, and so tall that the greatest enterprises of common men seem insignificant from your lofty perspective. With your mind as high as Mt. Fuji you can see all things clearly, and you can see all the forces that shape events; not just the things happening near you." – Miyamoto Musashi

"Do the difficult things while they are easy and do the great things while they are small. A journey of a thousand miles must begin with a single step." – Lao Tzu

"Embracing weakness keeps you weak. But enduring weakness can give you a kind of strength. You gain the will to get stronger." – Author

Mental fortitude is a test that everyone goes through when things get heated.It's a test to see if you stand in silence or stand up in confrontation to the matter. It is to have a resilient mind that dissolves worry and hesitation within you to be the better person in a difficult situation.

Mental Fortitude Is Having The Strength To Speak Up

Men today desperately need that push that makes them stand on their own feet and communicate with a voice like thunder. Their real at-home voice that has been beaten back into them through the highly female-oriented school system. Most guys like myself didn't start off shy and quiet, they were conditioned to obey which in turn makes us feel like we don't have any type of power to change anything significant within ourselves or anyone else. That idea weakens your strength to act when it's time to stand up for yourself or your friends.

A king never murmurs his words when he speaks to someone. He is confident and level headed to every social situation he is in, so he can make smart and rational decisions for the best possible outcomes. A king is someone who is in complete control of their mind, complete control of their actions, and complete control of their journey through life without being aggressive or manipulative to other people.

How do you think shy people come about? What makes many men today stay so shy and others more extroverted? Now you could say that thats just how some people were brought up, but in my opinion, these men have been knocked down mentally one too many times (too many bad days) so they retreat back into their comfort zones where it is very easy to either seek "alternatives" for reconnection (Video games, constant social media use, procrastination) or seek isolationism where they are more likely to succumb to addiction and loneliness which could lead to suicide.

"He who has a why to live for can bear anyhow" – Friedrich Nietzsche

11

Detox Your Overstimulated Brain

Create a time in your day, at least for 1 solid hour where you're bored. Be absolutely bored with yourself. **Boredom** is the 1 thing that I've learned we all needed as kids, so we can think about what we really want to do in the future, and create a path of **purpose** that leads towards our goal as we grow older. But because it was addictive to look into the screen for instant gratification and entertainment for hours every single day with parents that have the same problems, we have fried our young brains so much that we are bored but **without purpose,** and without a goal that we strive to achieve. This huge ultra-fast advancement of technology has been our generation's doom. The 'boomer's' had a point when they said to, "get off the phone and play outside", now they are almost gone and soon it will be our time to rule the world. If we still haven't disconnected ourselves from the internet regularly, it truly will be over for the planet.

A daily dopamine detox rewires your brain by exchanging the pleasure found on social media with delayed gratification that provides meaningful ventures. The detox strategy removes harmful elements and edifies your life with healthy habits fit for a king.

I recommend challenging yourself with a 24 hour dopamine detox and next a 30 day challenge to help remove your internet addictions. (Even if you can't escape from screens or music at work or shopping, don't worry because you only need to focus on what **you** can control).
The 24 hour rules are:

- No electronics of any type (Phone, Computer, video games,etc.)
- No music

- No Masturbation or sex
- No TV or movies
- No coffee or energy stimulants
- No reading of books,magazines or newspapers
- The 30 day rules are:
- Uninstall all social media
- Avoid Multitasking, do 1 task at a time
- Consistent Meditation
- Journaling Exercises
- Turn off notifications
- Go outside and touch grass everyday

"Life is not a quest for pleasure or a quest for power, but a quest for meaning"
– Viktor E. Frankl

6

Build The Starting Barriers Against Negative Energy

I n order to actually make progress with rebuilding your broken mental fortifications, you must first **acknowledge** all of your bad habits and face them head on, even the ones that you know make you procrastinate or the "fun" habits that you'd think are fine but are really just a coping mechanism to escape reality and waste time.

Now I understand that when people are addicted to something that has long term negative effects, they are no longer in control of themselves. Meditation can help with thought control but the addiction itself will always be there until you stop feeding it completely over a sufficient period of time. Even when we're going through the withdrawal phase, and it seems that we've conquered it, we haven't, it's just lying dormant waiting for the right time to strike. That is why you need to take certain precautions to handle the problem effectively.

Your Environment Fuels Your Cravings

One way that helped me break my pornography addiction, was that I linked my craving to the usage of my phone and computer to my house, and said to myself that I would never use either of them inside the house, if I wanted to work on something that required them, I would have to go to the library or some other public space for it. It can literally be anywhere, as long as you know for a fact that you **cannot** feel the need to give in to your degrading sensations. This method only helps ease the addictive sensations but not permanently erase it, due to the fact that your brain is quite clever and will try to break you down during your most vulnerable time of day. That is at least for me; before I go outside or when it's time to go to sleep.

Track Your Progress

Track your progress daily in a notebook or journal to stay properly engaged in achieving the goals that you've set for yourself. This I believe is crucial because it actively challenges you to focus on smaller goals that you do today and tomorrow to get closer and closer to your main goal at the end. It makes you feel like you have a sense of **purpose**, something to strive and go all in for, and holds you accountable for any mistakes that hold you back. Without tracking your progress daily, it is very easy to fall back to the bottom, and I say this through almost a decade of experience. If I were to just keep all of my current progress in my head, I would then be relying on motivation and willpower, which may seem good at first but remember, motivation and willpower is just another **sensation**. It's made up of the same chemical formula that makes up the addiction itself, so the all-good pumped up feeling that I have at the moment will soon fade or give out which will lead me back to square one. Consistency will always be an arduous task sometimes, but if you remind yourself what the **purpose** of doing this is for, to be **1% better** everyday, it can soon create a **purpose** in life for you.

7

Reprogramming Your Brain

In my opinion, the reason why this process is so difficult to do consistently is because we don't have a proper **strategy** to deal with it effectively. How can you track your progress if you don't even have a plan in the first place? I recommended creating a **plan** to deal with bad mental health but do you still find yourself constantly failing in following your own system time in and time out? That means there are errors in the plan that should be revised, even if whatever was written down could ultimately help, you need to restructure by filling in the times when you are weakest to bad habits and **replacing** those times with a positive habit to counteract before you do the misdeed.Keep in mind that one of the reasons for reorganizing your brain in the first place is to also (in my personal case) get rid of any mental **conditioning** that was brought upon you, making you have habits that seem like they happen automatically in your routine.That 'automatic bad habit' nature that we all dealt with can cease entirely by being accustomed to your behavioral patterns.

"Concern should drive us into action and not into a depression. No man is free who cannot control himself."- Pythagoras

"I never did anything worth doing by accident, nor did any of my inventions come by accident; they came by work - Plato

If you don't want to be a slave to your mind. First, stop acting like a slave to your mind. - Author

Practice Self-Love

Do you love yourself?
  Do you love the way you treat yourself?
  What does self-love mean to you?
  How does hating yourself benefit you or anyone else?

Ask yourself these questions **verbally** while you are directly facing a wall. Remember, actual love isn't something that lasts a day, week, month, or year. "Love" is full appreciation through actions that support the growth of one's physical, psychological, and spiritual nature in the highest regard. Self-love means not settling for less than what you truly deserve. Being happy in second place is only fine when in a competition with other people, but this is a competition with who really **controls you**. Being second place is **never an option** when the well-being of the mind is at stake. I understand that we all take care of ourselves differently, but the end goal is always the same, love of oneself. Don't do it because you "need to" or "have to", do it out of sheer **respect** for your body and mind. You are worth **a lot** more than you think you do.

Tips to start off with:

- Talking to yourself positively
- Forgiving yourself for bad deeds
- Be mindful of automatic behavior and turn away from it (immediately sitting on the couch after work, eating large unhealthy meals, smoking or drinking etc)
- Have a responsibility that you must uphold if you don't have one already (taking care of a friend,pet,guardian,kids etc.)
- Be true to yourself, don't do things that sacrifice your well-being to please others

"It is during our darkest moments that we must focus to see the light" - Aristotle

"A king in my view is no different from gigachad, he exists so men can strive to be a better man than they were yesterday". – Author

Get a Hobby

In order to reprogram your mind, you must focus on **substituting** bad habits with good ones, so that eventually you'll be addicted to things that can greatly help you instead of hurt you. But to stay consistent at it, you must create a personal strategy that you can look back on everyday to make sure you stay on the right track.The feeling that you could also be lacking, is **willpower**. Ask yourself "Do I have the will to obtain my crown"? The answer will **always** be "yes", if you continue to fight and never give up on yourself. If nobody is there to hold you accountable for your own actions at the moment, then you have to be the one to be responsible for yourself to become a stronger person mentally and physically.

Great hobbies that can anyone can implement anytime in their life:

- Riding a bike or jogging
- Painting and Drawing
- Reading books and putting the knowledge that you now learned for self-benefit
- Cooking for yourself or someone
- Hiking
- Hunting etc.

There are so many other hobbies out there, all you have to do is pick one and go for it. Your mind will begin to clean itself out and you will start to enjoy the good side of life that has been missing from countless people for way too long now.

Start Training

Whether starting out in the gym or at home as a beginner is a challenge for everyone. It may seem impossible to train consistently at first thought, but once you get through week 1 of training, the hard routine quickly becomes a fun habit that builds great **confidence** and **strength** to the body and mind over the months. I recommend weight/calisthenics training 3 days a week minimum, everyone has at least 1 hour of free time that they can dedicate towards a healthy lifestyle. There are **no excuses** for this. Basically all you have to do is:

- Buy or make a training schedule
- Focus on training two muscle groups per workout.

- Write down the specific weight, sets, and reps that you can currently do properly and set a realistic goal.
- Do a small 5-10 minute warm up before a workout and stretch after a workout.
- Start pushing yourself every workout day and week to achieve your goal.

Unfortunately, many people give up training before they really begin. The biggest mistakes I see most people do online when first starting out is that they:

- **Over exert** themselves on the first day, and ultimately end up quitting on the first week.
- Get way too **over confident** for way too long which quickly starts to work against them rather than for them. (ego lifting for attention)
- Are not pushing themselves enough, and/or they are never **challenging their muscles** with the proper weight for growth.
- Are training for more than an hour or going to the gym everyday. **(over training)**
- Have **Improper form** with weights. (can cause serious injury)
- Don't track their progress or have a training schedule. (no organization)

"No man has the right to be an amateur in the matter of physical training. It is a shame for a man to grow old without seeing the beauty and strength of which his body is capable" - Socrates

8

The Wants And Needs Of Spending

L ook around your living space for 1 minute and ask yourself how much stuff you use on a daily or weekly basis. Is your house/apartment cluttered with things that you rarely use? How many times have you felt buyers regret?

The modern 21st century man has a huge problem with spending large amounts of money on useless junk that could have been better used just sitting in his savings account. From my experience, my parents' financial doctrine is if something is broken, even if it could be fixed with a screw or it requires you to be a bit creative to fix it, they just tossed it and bought a brand new one even for items that cost over 100$. Now my parents could afford to do this countless times without much thought but let me tell you that that is one of the worst things you can ever do with money. My mom once told me that as a little girl she wished to be rich, but in all honesty, she could have actually been rich if she realized and corrected her bad spending habits. Unfortunately the west's huge love for buying material products en masse have taken over so many people's minds, that now they can't enjoy the same freedom that they've naively taken for granted.

Minimalism

Minimalism is a lifestyle that has sprung into popularity in recent years for its simple and inexpensive living doctrine of prioritizing essentials as a means to save more money and declutter the house. It is a fairly easy way to change your living standards with the added bonus of being organized and having more space in your rooms. With inflation getting higher and higher, there isn't a good enough reason to not adopt a modest living standard, the only "downside" to it is that you can't buy the things you want, but what you 'want' is "technically" a waste of money. For example: In my opinion, video games are a waste of money that people buy to waste their time (unless you actively make money playing them or you are financially free) and fills unnecessary space in the house all in the name of dopamine hits. I'm not saying that you shouldn't have fun, but becoming a minimalist means that you have to direct your focus on the things that you **need** rather than **want**.

People **could** critique this by saying, "minimalism makes the house look boring and unlively." I would ask them this, "would you have a home filled with everything that you want or outfitted with everything that you need." The space in which you live could be relative to that of your fortified/unfortified mind. It is obvious that the mind works better when it isn't filled with junk that was never important to begin with, which is exactly the kind of situation where it is constantly stressed, leading to all the bad things that I've said before. Converting to a minimalist lifestyle is a serious one no doubt, but so unbelievably **relieving** that your one simple decision cleaned up your entire house. Now you just need to keep it that way (which is very easy).

9

The Cruciality Of Time Management

"Worthless people live only to eat and drink; people of worth eat and drink only to live."- Socrates

Imagine if you compared your wasted time to that of a man of the same age just 80 or 50 years ago. The potential of a single man in any age, even our own, is absolutely enormous; we can really achieve our dreams or the dreams of our fathers if our time was dedicated to it. Do we understand that time is of utmost importance, even if millions of us waste entire decades on instant gratifying material, the time when we are productive and hard working is valued to the highest degree in our lives. When you really think about it, time is all we have, and depending on what you do with that time, can make you or break you. It's as simple as that.

"Let us postpone nothing."— Seneca

Procrastination

Are you consciously aware of your productivity when you're being productive?

Or are you consciously aware that you're procrastinating when you're procrastinating? Notice how you feel in your mind when choosing to be productive eventually pays off, and how "doing it tomorrow" just wastes 24 hours with no gain or benefit. From a personal standpoint, I admit that I still procrastinate even when I have plenty of free hours that could've went into fulfilling my goals, but I understand that fortifying the mind is a **journey** with many faults and traps, I have to fall into to fully understand my own imperfections so that tomorrow I can learn to correct the choices I make.

Talking about procrastination as an adult, ultimately just goes back to talking about **instant gratification** and **delayed gratification** because that's exactly what it comes down to. You need to be **more than willing** to sacrifice today's comfort for future happiness and financial stability. There are no excuses, in reality we as human beings have **plenty of time and plenty of options** to get the type of life that we want (in the western world), it's just that in the 21st century, having more time and options than we ever had in history scares us so much that we end up giving that precious resource either to other people that don't have our best interests in mind, or modern pleasures which make us more isolated and reclusive than ever before. When you procrastinate, you are delaying the inevitable and because you delayed it, the negative impact will hit a lot harder when it could have been avoided. In all honesty, procrastination is just another term for laziness that must be reduced as much as possible.

Fortify your mental walls now, or let yourself crumble for years to come. It is never too late to become the sole ruler of your mind because that's how this journey was intended, to be a struggle against the odds. There is always **plenty of time** for you to turn around to set things straight the way you would like to set things straight.

"The man who says he can, and the man who says he can not. Are both correct".
– Confucius

10

The Kingdom Of Self-Discipline

"Most People... Are like a falling leaf that drifts and turns in the air, flutters, and falls to the ground. But a few others are like stars which travel one defined path: No wind reaches them. They have within themselves their guide and path." – Herman Hesse

"Victory belongs to the most persevering" – Napoleon Bonaparte

"The ideal man bears the accidents of life with dignity and grace, making the best of circumstances"- Aristotle

Every idea that was included in this book relates to achieving discipline and the steps to find an easier path to mindful fortification in the face of extreme hardship. By choosing to act on improving yourself when life seems to be going downhill, you're actively forcing your brain to be disciplined, by doing something that you didn't want to do.

Achieving discipline in oneself is the **prime key** that unlocks the wisdom of the entire self-improvement hierarchy of **purpose**. In my opinion, "**purpose**" is the most important of all. You need **purpose** to get out of bed, you need **purpose** to go outside and touch grass, you need **purpose** to go to the gym and do 3 sets of Bulgarian squats on a leg day. Conquering the faults of the mind through self-discipline will awaken your lost ambitious drive to be in a significantly greater position than you are today.

This idea is one of the reasons that strong militaries in the age of kingdoms and empires efficiently conquered their enemies even when they were greatly outnumbered or outmatched on the battlefield. They became highly respected by their foes and allies alike if they managed to face it head on securing a **victory**. Those men had to harden their minds in countless battles to be praised and recognized for their high sense of professionalism, willpower, and strength. Their life had meaning even when their lives were used as if it didn't. Their personal goal was to achieve **victory** and later settle down in peace and quiet. Those days may be centuries apart from our own but the idea of war never did; you see, in order for men to win a war, they first need to win a war in their minds.

We are all going through the same thing they did all those years ago, but instead of a physical war it's a psychological one. We can only lose if we give up on ourselves, and win through **purpose** and working smarter instead of harder. I need you to realize a purpose for yourself. A **purpose** that makes you a king in your own right, with a **fortified** castle wall so that your kingdom, which is your own mind, doesn't break down through the hard times.

"He who has a why to live for can bear anyhow" – *Friedrich Nietzsche*

The battles that were fought and won with swords and muskets, must first be fought and won with restraint and mindfulness." – *Author*

11

Resources

Scott. (2021, July 29). *17 Highly Effective Stress Relievers*. Verywell Mind. Retrieved May 23, 2022, from https://www.verywellmind.com/tips-to-reduce-stress-3145195
https://www.verywellmind.com/tips-to-reduce-stress-3145195

Suni, E. (2022, May 13). *Sleep Statistics*. Sleep Foundation. Retrieved May 23, 2022, from https://www.sleepfoundation.org/how-sleep-works/sleep-facts-statistics
https://www.sleepfoundation.org/how-sleep-works/sleep-facts-statistics

Mitchell, R. (2021, November 3). *Dopamine Detox – Fix Your Brain and Survive Modern Life With a Dopamine Fast*. The Tiny Life. https://thetinylife.com/dopamine-detox-fix-your-brain-and-survive-modern-life-

with-a-dopamine-fast/#:%7E:text=24-Hr%20Dopamine%20Detox%20
Rules%201%20No%20electronics%20of,or%20movies%207%20No%20
Coffee%20or%20other%20stimulants

https://thetinylife.com/dopamine-detox-fix-your-brain-and-survi
ve-modern-life-with-a-dopamine-fast/#:~:text=24-Hr%20Dopamin
e%20Detox%20Rules%201%20No%20electronics%20of,or%20movies
%207%20No%20Coffee%20or%20other%20stimulants

American Foundation For Suicide Prevention. (2022, February 28).
Suicide statistics. Retrieved May 23, 2022, from https://afsp.org/suicide
-statistics/

https://afsp.org/suicide-statistics/

Borenstein. (2020, July 9). *Self-Love and What It Means.* Brain &
Behavior Research Foundation. Retrieved May 23, 2022, from https://w
ww.bbrfoundation.org/blog/self-love-and-what-it-means

https://www.bbrfoundation.org/blog/self-love-and-what-it-mean
s

Skidmore. (n.d.). *Study.com | Take Online Courses. Earn College Credit.
Research Schools, Degrees & Careers.* Study.Com. Retrieved March 23,
2022, from https://study.com/learn/lesson/what-is-self-discipline.ht
ml

https://study.com/learn/lesson/what-is-self-discipline.html

Help, H. (2021, May 3). *100+ Creative & Fun Hobbies to Try - Ultimate
List 2022.* Hobby Help. Retrieved May 23, 2022, from https://hobbyhel
p.com/inspiration/list-of-hobbies/

https://hobbyhelp.com/inspiration/list-of-hobbies/

Printed in Great Britain
by Amazon